Schiffer Publishing

International Award Winning

POOLS, SPAS, & WATER ENVIRONMENTS IV

Joseph A. Vassallo, Mary Vail, and Joseph M. Vassallo

Presented by GAVA

Schiffer Publishing Ltd
4880 Lower Valley Road • Atglen, PA 19310

Other Schiffer Books by the Author:
International Award Winning Pools, Spas and Water Environments, 978-0-7643-3480-1, $24.99
International Award Winning Pools, Spas, & Water Environments II, 978-0-7643-3802-1, $34.99
International Award Winning Pools, Spas, & Water Environments III, 978-0-7643-4102-1, $34.99

Library of Congress Control Number: 2012956156

Cover and book designed by John P. Cheek
Type set in Optima Nova LT

ISBN: 978-0-7643-4408-4
Printed in China

Provisio: Information and images submitted for a GAVA were provided by the entrant. Entrants certified that all information, data and images submitted for the GAVA awards and the publication is accurate and factual. All images were provided by the entrants with the full cooperation and authorized releases. Three V Enterprises, GAVA, its representatives, the publishers, and sponsors are not responsible or liable for any misleading or inaccurate data or images contained in this publication.

Published by Schiffer Publishing, Ltd.
4880 Lower Valley Road
Atglen, PA 19310
Phone: (610) 593-1777; Fax: (610) 593-2002
E-mail: *Info@schifferbooks.com*

In Europe, Schiffer books are distributed by
Bushwood Books
6 Marksbury Ave.
Kew Gardens
Surrey TW9 4JF England
Phone: 44 (0) 20 8392 8585; Fax: 44 (0) 20 8392 9876
E-mail: info@bushwoodbooks.co.uk
Website: www.bushwoodbooks.co.uk

ACKNOWLEDGMENTS

Three V Enterprises acknowledges those who support GAVA's vision. Our appreciation goes to the following organizations and their staff for their continued sponsorship and endorsement:

Structure Studios: Noah Nehlich, Stephanie Dunn, J.R. Rapp, and Ross Horvitz;

Zodiac: Vance Gillette, Scott Frost, Michelle Baldwin, and Tessa McHenry;

Paramount Pool Systems: Buzz Ghiz and Bill Burt;

Pebble Technology, Inc. Interior Finishes: Bob Haning;

The Schiffer Publishing Team;

Our editorial assistants: Sean Ammerman and Ashley Vail;

And, to our supportive spouses: Alana and Dave

GAVA
GLOBAL AQUATEKTURE VISIONARY AWARDS
WINNER

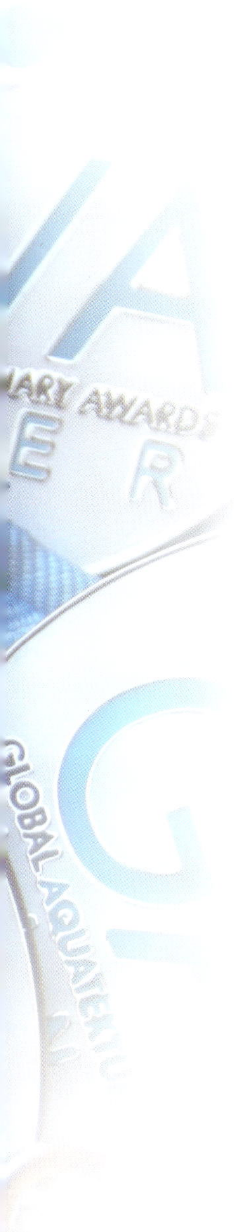

CONTENTS

ABOUT THE GAVA

GAVA recognizes artisans globally whose visions and creativity exemplify the best in AquaTekture: the discipline of designing, engineering, and erecting water environments and ancillary components in a harmonious nature with consideration to function, space, and aesthetics.

Transcending beyond the traditional water-themed design awards GAVA hosts an integrated world-wide competition open to design professionals of all genres dedicated to influencing and creating thought-provoking solutions.

WHAT INSPIRES A GAVA-WINNING VISIONARY?

Is it the vista, rock boulders, the jungle, art, tile, fire, glass panels, music, the shore line, or the night sky? Perhaps it is the challenge of harnessing nature's most prized element- water; or rather a combination of both.

Whatever the source of inspiration, each of these GAVA winners were tasked to craft a one-of-a-kind setting. The result is a compilation of thought-provoking works of AquaTekture that fuse the lines between function, design and art.

Each collaborated with a team of professionals that provided them with the tools, talents, resources, products, and expertise to achieve their goal.

This diverse and international group of artisans has fulfilled the dreams and exceeded the expectations of its cultured clients. The award-winning collection includes a ranchland watering hole, a personal water park, a jungle-themed spa, a moat, dancing fountains, and a mythical mermaid.

GAVA

GLOBAL AQUATEKTURE VISIONARY AWARDS™

THE COMPETITION

The competition acknowledges the most innovative concepts, designs, materials, and applications of water-inspired environments from across the globe in commercial use, mixed use, hospitality, public use, recreational and residential use, in both interior and exterior applications.

GAVA is the only independent design awards competition open to all design disciplines: architects, contractors, interior and exterior designers, home builders, pool builders, and landscape architects and designers worldwide.

Categories include pools, spas, water features, lakes, waterfalls, reflection ponds, koi ponds, and water fountains, as well as special materials such as lighting, acrylic walls, tiles, art, natural materials and "green" AquaTekture.

Presenting Sponsor, Structure Studios, bestows the GAVA-Structure Studios Award to artisans who have created exceptional AquaTekture. This category recognizes the compelling power and elegance of designs imagined with Structure Studios' Instant 3D technology as well as for design innovativeness.

GAVA winning applications were presented in three levels; Gold, Silvor, and Bronze. GAVA Gold winners receive a crystal water drop trophy.

PHILANTHROPIC ENDEAVORS

As part of 3VE's commitment to enhance philanthropic endeavors worldwide, a special program was established specifically to assist with the financial limitations of non-profit organizations. The program extends to any qualifying entity, such as a religious building, educational institution, fitness center, or popular attraction site such as museums, aquariums, animal parks, and zoos. Entries can be submitted into any of the many categories, including pools, spas, water features, waterfalls, reflection ponds, koi ponds, animal habitats, and water fountains.

Three V Enterprises also provides funding as part of its comprehensive philosophical and philanthropic objectives. All proceeds from the sale of *International Award-Winning Pools, Spas, & Water Environments* series go toward the fund.

Support from GAVA sponsors – Structure Studios, Zodiac, Paramount Pool and Spa Systems, and Pebble Technology, Inc. – allows 3VE to provide these philanthropic programs. Additional information is available at www.gavaawards.com

Section One

RESIDENTIAL AQUATEKTURE

GOLD AWARD WINNER

POOL ENVIRONMENTS

CATEGORY
Traditional

PROJECT
Serene
Dallas, Texas, USA
18 feet x 36 feet

Photos courtesy of Graham Hobart.

THE VISIONARIES

BUILDER
Pool Environments
www.poolenvironments.com
972.985.1576
Plano, Texas, USA
Association of Pool and Spa Professionals

DESIGNER
Randy Angell, Pool Environments

THE VISION

The vision was to create a quiet oasis in the midst of a very busy city. Multiple elevations, strategic lighting and water features were incorporated to create a serene environment.

The main focal point of the project is a water wall featuring four ten-foot vertical channels tiled with Bisazza glass tile. Flanked on either side are two Sheer Descent waterfalls on raised planters. A separate elevated spa features a water wall.

FEATURES
Zodiac Pool Systems, Inc.

GOLD AWARD WINNER

AQUASCAPE

CATEGORY
Traditional

PROJECT
Villa Belvedere
Belvedere, California, USA
14 feet x 50 feet

Photos courtesy of Greg Gardea Photography.

THE VISIONARIES

BUILDER
Aquascape
www.aquascape.org
707.769.7212
Petaluma, California, USA
Association of Pool and Spa Professionals

ARCHITECT
Walker & Moody Architects
www.walkermoody.com

CONTRACTOR
Cello & Maudru Construction Company
www.cello-maudru.com

THE VISION

This project originally started thirty years ago before being abandoned for twenty years. Working with the architects, the new owners redesigned the entire site with a new pool. The vision was to take advantage of the natural terrain of the cliff-side estate. This was achieved by designing a large water wall that flows down towards a raised spa just feet away from the all-tile pool.

FEATURES
Zodiac Pool Systems, Inc.

SILVOR
AWARDWINNER

ALOHA POOLS PTY LTD

CATEGORY
Traditional

PROJECT
Ornamental Elegance
Brighton, Victoria, Australia
13.06 meters x 3.53 meters
(42'11" x 11'7")

Photos courtesy of George Kochukudiyil.

THE VISIONARIES

BUILDER

Aloha Pools Pty Ltd
www.alohapools.com.au
03.9775.0033
Carrum Downs, Victoria, Australia
Swimming Pool & Spa Association of Victoria
Paramount Advisory Committee Enterprise

DESIGNER

Paul Bangay Design
www.paulbangay.com

THE VISION

The clients wanted a pool that would complement the outdoor entertaining area. The vision was to have a landscape design to look at the property as a whole and to ensure that all of the individual elements, including the pool, worked together to form a beautiful outdoor space. The pool is close enough to the house to be functional for entertaining yet stands alone as a visual feature. Bisazza glass mosaic tiles make the water sparkle with an icy clarity.

FEATURES

Paramount Pool & Spa Systems

SILVOR AWARD WINNER

STONECREST POOLS

CATEGORY
Traditional

PROJECT
Private Ranch in Texas
Dallas, Texas, USA
119 feet x 30 feet

Photos courtesy of Sean Gallagher.

THE VISIONARIES

BUILDER/CONTRACTOR
StoneCrest Pools
www.stonecrestpools.com
817.988.2941
Keller, Texas, USA
Association of Pool and Spa Professionals
Genesis3 Gold Member

DESIGNER
Doug Johnston, StoneCrest Pools

THE VISION

The vision was to create an elegant design that would also be entertaining for multiple generations of poolgoers. The pool features an all-glass tile interior, four underwater speakers, two custom-made pool covers for safety, thirty-seven LED lights, and fountain heads. Taking center stage is an elevated tiled platform that houses the extravagant fountain and lighting display, which can be synchronized to music.

FEATURES
Designed with Structure Studios 3-D Pool Studio

BRONZE
AWARD WINNER

AQUASCAPE

CATEGORY
Traditional

PROJECT
Dry Creek Valley
Healdsburg, California, USA
20 feet x 75 feet

Photos courtesy of Greg Gardea Photography.

THE VISIONARIES

BUILDER
Aquascape
www.aquascape.org
707.769.7212
Petaluma, California, USA
Association of Pool and Spa Professionals

ARCHITECT
Backen, Gillam & Kroeger Architects
www.bgarch.com

CONTRACTOR
Ledcor Group of Companies
www.ledcor.com

THE VISION

The vision was to keep the design simple and allow the environment to be the showpiece. The raised pool was built on forty piers and required fifteen feet of fill to establish a level pad to support it.

FEATURES
Zodiac Pool Systems, Inc.

BRONZE AWARDWINNER

TEXAS POOLS

CATEGORY
Traditional

PROJECT
Ketchum
The Woodlands, Texas, USA
989 square feet

THE VISIONARIES

BUILDER/CONTRACTOR
Texas Pools
www.texaspools.com
281.367.4660
The Woodlands, Texas, USA
Association of Pool and Spa Professionals
American Society of Interior Designers
National Association of Home Builders

DESIGNER
Paul Ryan, Texas Pools

THE VISION

The vision was to design a simple, traditional pool that had no vertical obstructions of the nearby scenery. The spa sits completely inside the beam of the pool and features a negative edge on the front and back sides. The rear of the pool also features a negative edge that is framed by two pedestals and planter pots. The water spills into a catch basin at the foot of the wraparound stairs. Opposing bubblers create vertical movement to an otherwise smooth surface. The classic travertine tile and decking add an old-world feel to the project.

FEATURES
Designed with Structure Studios 3-D Pool Studio
Pebble Technology, Inc. Pool Finishes
Paramount Pool & Spa Systems

Photos courtesy of Texas Pools.

GOLD AWARDWINNER

THE SWIMMING MAN

CATEGORY
Natural Setting

PROJECT
Texas Hill Country
Ranch Pool
Wimberley, Texas, USA
18 feet x 48 feet

Photos courtesy of Greg Smith.

THE VISIONARIES

BUILDER/DESIGNER
Greg Smith, The Swimming Man
www.theswimmingman.com
512.844.6263
Austin, Texas, USA
Society of Watershape Designers

PROJECT OWNER:
Luciano Ranch

THE VISION

The vision was to create a pool that replicated the surrounding hill country terrain of the client's ranch property. The result is a pond that looks as if it is the work of "Mother Nature" rather than crafted by man.

Large flat rocks were stacked around the pool creating multi-elevations representative of the hill side. Resonating with the wild fowl that reside on the ranch, a flock of turkey comes to the pool to drink in the evenings.

FEATURES
Designed with Structure Studios 3-D Pool Studio
Zodiac Pool Systems, Inc.
Pebble Technology, Inc. Pool Finishes
Paramount Pool & Spa Systems

SILVOR AWARDWINNER

ALDERETE POOLS, INC.

CATEGORY
Natural Setting

PROJECT
Hans
Orange County, California, USA
22 feet x 40 feet

Photos courtesy of Alderete Pools, Inc.

THE VISIONARIES

BUILDER/DESIGNER/CONTRACTOR

Alderete Pools, Inc.
www.alderetepools.com
800.492.7289
San Clemente, California, USA
Association of Pool and Spa Professionals

THE VISION

A natural setting was the vision for this spa, pool, waterfall, and koi pond. Natural stone was incorporated into the decking, coping, spa dam wall, and boulder waterfall. A custom wood bridge and full size fireplace enrich the natural setting.

FEATURES

Paramount Pool & Spa Systems
All-tile Interior

GOLD AWARDWINNER

BLUE STONE POOLS

CATEGORY
Infinity Edge Pool

PROJECT
Wellington Street
Mosman Park,
Western Australia, Australia
15 meters x 3 meters
(49′2″ x 9′10″)

Photos courtesy of Giorgi Exclusive Homes.

THE VISIONARIES

CONTRACTOR

Blue Stone Pools
www.bluestonepools.com.au
08.9249.6647
Malaga, Western Australia, Australia
Association of Pool and Spa Professionals
Master Builders Association of Australia

ARCHITECT

Giorgi Exclusive Architectural
www.giogiexclusivehomes.com.au

DESIGNERS:

Mark Rietveld, Giorgi Exclusive Homes
Grant Osborne, Blue Stone Pools

PROJECT OWNER:

Freind Residence

THE VISION

With the home situated on a cliff face overlooking the river and city skyline, the vision was to create an infinity edge that blended seamlessly into the river's horizon. The pool and spa are meant to be seen from indoors but careful planning was done to ensure they do not disrupt any views from other parts of the open plan home. This was achieved by creating different entertaining levels around the pool. The pool water is all purified and harvested from underground tanks. Water heating is done via solar pool matting while the power for pool equipment is harnessed by electric solar panels.

GOLD
AWARD WINNER

ALL AMERICAN CUSTOM POOLS & SPAS, INC.

CATEGORY
Infinity Edge

PROJECT
Bieder
Pound Ridge, New York, USA
828 square feet

Photos courtesy of All American Custom Pools & Spas, Inc.

THE VISIONARIES

BUILDER/DESIGNER

All American Custom Pools & Spas, Inc.
www.allamericanpools.com
203.847.2704
Norwalk, Connecticut, USA
Association of Pool and Spa Professionals

PROJECT OWNER:

Richard Bieder

THE VISION

The vision was to construct a pool on a sloping backyard property for both the children and adults to enjoy. Excavation for the pool, plumbing and equipment room required chipping out solid rock. This challenging project was completed during a cold New York winter and required the use of more than ten 100-gallon propane tanks for heating.

FEATURES

Zodiac Pool Systems, Inc.
Pebble Technology, Inc. Pool Finishes

GOLD AWARD WINNER

STONECREST POOLS

CATEGORY
Infinity Edge

PROJECT
Thompson
Mansfield, Texas, USA
260 feet perimeter

Photos courtesy of Sean Gallagher.

THE VISIONARIES

BUILDER/CONTRACTOR
StoneCrest Pools
www.stonecrestpools.com
817.988.2941
Keller, Texas, USA
Association of Pool and Spa Professionals
Genesis3 Gold Member

DESIGNER
Doug Johnston, StoneCrest Pools

PROJECT OWNER:
Thompson Residence

THE VISION

The vision was to design an elegant pool that would reflect the trees surrounding the property. The pool features ninety feet of infinity edge, glass tile, a perimeter overflow raised spa, fire bowls, and dual swim-up bars.

FEATURES
Designed with Structure Studios 3-D Pool Studio

SILVOR AWARDWINNER

ALL AMERICAN CUSTOM POOLS & SPAS, INC.

CATEGORY
Infinity Edge

PROJECT
Mechanic
Pound Ridge, New York, USA
1,000 square feet

Photos courtesy of All American Custom Pools & Spas, Inc.

THE VISIONARIES

BUILDER/DESIGNER
All American Custom Pools & Spas, Inc.
www.allamericanpools.com
203.847.2704
Norwalk, Connecticut, USA
Association of Pool and Spa Professionals

PROJECT OWNER:
Jeffery Mechanic

THE VISION

The vision was to create a unique outdoor living space. In addition to the infinity edge, the pool area features a large wet deck, multiple laminar deck jets, a lap lane and a raised spa with a waterfall. The expansive entertaining area includes a built-in barbecue, a fire bowl and plenty of seating space.

FEATURES
Zodiac Pool Systems, Inc.
Pebble Technology, Inc. Pool Finishes

SILVOR AWARDWINNER

AQUA BLUE POOLS

CATEGORY
Infinity Edge

PROJECT
Oberwellyn Residence
Pacific Palisades, California, USA
18 feet x 36 feet

THE VISIONARIES

BUILDER/CONTRACTOR
Aqua Blue Pools
www.aquabluecreations.com
805.499.0972
Newbury Park, California, USA
ASSOCIATION OF POOL AND SPA PROFESSIONALS

ARCHITECT/DESIGNER
Ken Ungar Architect
www.kenungararchitect.com

PROJECT OWNER:
Oberwellyn Residence

THE VISION

The vision was to build a pool with a simplistic design and clean lines. The construction was done on a hillside, which required six caissons to be installed fifty feet deep into the earth for support. The pool features an automatic cover with a hidden leading edge design. This was a challenge to build due to the pool's unique infinity edge.

FEATURES
Zodiac Pool Systems, Inc.

Photos courtesy of Aqua Blue Pools.

SILVOR AWARDWINNER

DISTINGUISHED POOLS, INC.

CATEGORY
Infinity Edge

PROJECT
Sweeping Views
San Diego, California, USA
20 feet x 40 feet

THE VISIONARIES

BUILDER/DESIGNER/CONTRACTOR
Dan Ramos
Distinguished Pools, Inc.
www.distinguishedpools.com
858.204.1532
Poway, California, USA
Association of Pool and Spa Professionals

THE VISION

The vision was to showcase the home's architecture and accent the sweeping views of the mountains in the distance. Modular stone tiles were fabricated and painstakingly installed on the entire back of the vanishing edge wall before being carried into linear pieces for the waterline. The spa shares the vanishing edge wall with the pool. When the vanishing edge is turned on, the water gently pans out, creating a seamless 40-foot flow over the edge.

FEATURES
Zodiac Pool Systems, Inc.
Designed with Structure Studios 3-D Pool Studio

Photos courtesy of Darren Edwards.

BRONZE
AWARDWINNER

SUNSET POOLS

CATEGORY
Infinity Edge

PROJECT
South Coogee
South Coogee, New South Wales, Australia
12 meters x 3 meters
(39′4″ x 9′10″)

Photos courtesy of Mitch Cammeron Photography.

THE VISIONARIES

BUILDER/DESIGNER/CONTRACTOR

Sunset Pools
www.sunsetpools.com.au
1300.000.412
North Ryde, New South Wales, Australia
Association of Pool and Spa Professionals
Swimming Pool & Spa Association of Australia
Master Builders Association

PROJECT OWNER:

Lihan Lan

THE VISION

The vision was to have the pool interact with the amazing view of the nearby sea. Using a commercial method of construction, we double-formed and poured the pool and balance tank, which forms the roof to the downstairs guest room. The infinity edge captures the incredible ocean views and blends nature with this elegant man-made creation.

FEATURES

Zodiac Pool Systems, Inc.

GOLD AWARD WINNER

SELECTIVE DESIGNS LLC

CATEGORY
Perimeter Overflow

PROJECT
Reflections
Peachtree City, Georgia, USA
18 feet x 36 feet

Photos courtesy of Breest Photography.

THE VISIONARIES

BUILDER/CONTRACTOR
Selective Designs LLC
www.selectivedesigns.com
770.631.1550
Peachtree City, Georgia, USA
Association of Pool and Spa Professionals

DESIGNER
Shane LeBlanc, Selective Designs LLC

PROJECT OWNER:
Preacher Residence

THE VISION

The vision was to combine the home owner's dream of a water feature and a pool where the family can swim throughout the year. The location inspired the perimeter overflow system, which emits no sound by incorporating a non-surge tank with a unique jet black edge design where cascading water disappears into a three-eighths-inch slot. The raised perimeter overflow spa floats gently over the pool. The magic of a "walk-on-water" path to the spa is enhanced by the dramatic reflection of the sky due to the use of black PebbleTec Pebble Sheen.

FEATURES
Zodiac Pool Systems, Inc.
Pebble Technology, Inc. Pool Finishes

GOLD AWARD WINNER

DOWNUNDA AQUATIC ENVIRONMENTS

CATEGORY
Perimeter Overflow

PROJECT
Mathews
Magnolia, Texas, USA
40 feet x 20 feet

THE VISIONARIES

BUILDER/CONTRACTOR
Downunda Aquatic Environments
www.downundapools.com
281.236.4344
Houston, Texas, USA
Association of Pool and Spa Professionals
American Society of Landscape Architects
National Association of Home Builders

DESIGNER
Brett Hatfield, Downunda Aquatic Environments

PROJECT OWNER:
Mathews residence

THE VISION

The vision for the project was to capitalize on the view of this waterfront property. Combining the components of a negative edge and a slot pool design creates uninterrupted surface water. The sunken entertainment area with a granite counter top allows guests to sit poolside with swimmers.

FEATURES
Designed with Structure Studios 3-D Pool Studio
Pebble Technology, Inc. Pool Finishes

Photos courtesy of Downunda Aquatic Environments.

SILVOR AWARD WINNER

POOL ENVIRONMENTS

CATEGORY
Perimeter Overflow

PROJECT
Zen
Dallas, Texas, USA
13 feet x 37 feet

Photos courtesy of Graham Hobart.

THE VISIONARIES

BUILDER
Pool Environments
www.poolenvironments.com
972.985.1576
Plano, Texas, USA
Association of Pool and Spa Professionals

DESIGNERS:
Chris Polito, Pool Environments
Jeff Bargas, BHB Landscape Architects, www.bhbg.com

THE VISION

The client wanted a very clean, simple design so as to not compete with the surrounding landscape. The vision resulted in a perimeter overflow design that acts as a mirror, thus reflecting the surrounding environment. As with any perimeter overflow pool, the finish of the edge has to be perfectly level in order to create the clean, crisp overspill. The modern lines and materials continue the design theme of the home's interior, mimicking the high-end boutique hotels the couple frequents in their travels.

FEATURES
Paramount Pool & Spa Systems

GOLD AWARD WINNER

DA VIDA POOLS LLC

CATEGORY
Freeform

PROJECT
Bisset Court
Lakeway, Texas, USA
38 feet x 10-22 feet

Photos courtesy of Da Vida Pools LLC.

THE VISIONARIES

BUILDER/DESIGNER
Lisa North and Andre Del Re
Da Vida Pools LLC
www.davidapools.com
512.751.2693
Austin, Texas, USA
Association of Pool and Spa Professionals

THE VISION

The vision of this water environment was to create an entire outdoor experience for both day and night, entertaining and relaxing, summer and winter. The pool had to seamlessly integrate with the site topography and surroundings, working with the other features (decking, fire pit, stone benches). The design layout guides the eye across many focal points, including the beautiful view of the lake and mountains. The flow of guests and water had to be both functional and logical to connect the residence with the poolscape and the yard.

GOLD AWARD WINNER

VENEZOLANA DE PISCINAS I, C.A.

CATEGORY
Freeform

PROJECT
Tairous
Valencia, Venezuela,
South America
288 square feet

Photos courtesy of Pierre Tairous.

THE VISIONARIES

BUILDER/DESIGNER

Venezolana de Piscinas I, C.A.
www.venezolanadepiscinas.com
58.414.3593754
Valencia, Venezuela, South America

PROJECT OWNER:

Elias Tairous

THE VISION

The vision for this all-tile pool design was to incorporate a small oasis in the client's backyard. This was created with sheets of water, fiber optic lighting, river rock coping and dark slate decking. The array of colors provided by the fiber optic lighting makes the pool a real night show that pleases every evening on the patio, making this a favorite spot of the family.

FEATURES

Designed with Structure Studios 3-D Pool Studio
All-tile Interior

SILVOR AWARDWINNER

ALDERETE POOLS, INC.

CATEGORY
Freeform

PROJECT
Engels
Orange County, California, USA
15 feet x 30 feet

Photos courtesy of Alderete Pools, Inc.

THE VISIONARIES

BUILDER/DESIGNER/CONTRACTOR
Alderete Pools, Inc.
www.alderetepools.com
800.492.7289
San Clemente, California, USA
Association of Pool and Spa Professionals

THE VISION

Evening ambience was the vision for this design. The natural stone on the raised bond beam of the pool was chosen to match the front of the house. The custom, poured-in-place concrete bullnose coping softens the edge of the pool and spa while completing the transition to the beautiful chiseled travertine decking. The pool and spa feature LED multi-colored lights, enhancing the nightlife feel. A solid tile roof gazebo completes the experience and features outdoor heating with a full stone fireplace. The pool and spa also feature an eco-pool in-floor circulatory system and an ozone system by Paramount.

FEATURES
Paramount Pool & Spa Systems
Pebble Technology, Inc. Pool Finishes

SILVOR AWARDWINNER

SERENITY POOLS & OUTDOOR LIVING

CATEGORY
Freeform

PROJECT
Scott Total Backyard
Conroe, Texas, USA
520 square feet

Photos courtesy of Quik Pic's Portrait Studio.

THE VISIONARIES

BUILDER/CONTRACTOR
Serenity Pools & Outdoor Living
www.serenitycustompool.com
832.900.7946
Cypress, Texas, USA
Association of Pool and Spa Professionals
Greater Houston Builders Association

DESIGNER
Greg Channel, Serenity Pools & Outdoor Living

PROJECT OWNER:
Eric Scott

THE VISION

The vision was to create an outdoor retreat that allowed the clients to entertain their guests with a variety of activities. This backyard began as a swampy, rough terrain. Standing water and severe elevation changes made the area more of a naturescape than a place for relaxation. The homeowner challenged us with a vision incorporating a pool, spa, fire pit, outdoor kitchen, and patio cover that spanned most of the back of the existing home.

FEATURES
Pebble Technology, Inc. Pool Finishes

SILVOR AWARDWINNER

TRUE BLUE SWIMMING POOLS

CATEGORY
Freeform

PROJECT
Feng Shui
Bayside, New York, USA
20 feet x 40 feet

Photos courtesy of True Blue Swimming Pools.

THE VISIONARIES

BUILDER/DESIGNER

True Blue Swimming Pools
www.trueblueswimmingpools.com
631.757.7665
Dix Hills, New York, USA
Association of Pool and Spa Professionals

CONTRACTOR

Michael Truehart, True Blue Swimming Pools

THE VISION

The vision was to design according to a principle of the Chinese tradition of feng shui. The project is completely free of corners or edges and features a curved Gunite pool and spa, stacked stone wall, waterfall, Sheer Descents, deck jets and a custom made cedar bridge. The patio and stone wall coping is crafted of travertine marble.

FEATURES

Zodiac Pool Systems, Inc.
Pebble Technology, Inc. Pool Finishes

BRONZE
AWARD WINNER

COLLEY'S POOLS & SPAS

CATEGORY
Freeform

PROJECT
Private Retreat
Orchard Park, New York, USA
111 linear feet

THE VISIONARIES

BUILDER/DESIGNER
Colley's Pools & Spas
www.colleys.com
716.649.7640
Hamburg, New York, USA
Association of Pool and Spa Professionals

THE VISION

After taking a family vacation to Atlantis Paradise Island, the homeowners wanted to create an impressive pool destination right in their own backyard. This vision was brought to fruition by designing a freeform pool with an 8 x 13-foot beach entry and a grotto with a waterfall. The beach entry was an important feature not only for their children, but also for the dogs. The area was designed with entertaining and parties in mind.

FEATURES
Zodiac Pool Systems, Inc.
Paramount Pool & Spa Systems

Photos courtesy of Callen Photography.

GOLD
AWARD WINNER

POOL ENVIRONMENTS

CATEGORY
All-Tile

PROJECT
Seamless
Dallas, Texas, USA
534 square feet

Photos courtesy of Graham Hobart.

THE VISIONARIES

BUILDER

Pool Environments
www.poolenvironments.com
972.985.1576
Plano, Texas, USA
Association of Pool and Spa Professionals

DESIGNER

Randy Angell, Pool Environments

THE VISION

The beautiful estate already had a well-designed backyard by a prominent landscape architect. This included the upper spa area, which we had built for the previous owner. The vision presented by the new homeowner was to create a seamless design that integrated the new with the existing while remaining true to the original architect's vision. The new pool and existing spa were finished with an all-tile surface of custom glass mosaic tile to add a touch of elegance.

FEATURES

Zodiac Pool Systems, Inc.

GOLD AWARD WINNER

UNIVERSAL GROUP, INC.

CATEGORY
All-Tile

PROJECT
Hartford
Beverly Hills, California, USA
120 linear feet

THE VISIONARIES

BUILDER/DESIGNER/CONTRACTOR

Universal Group, Inc.
www.universalpoolandspa.com
800.957.6657
Reseda, California, USA

THE VISION

The vision was to design a multi-functional element incorporating design components of the home. The pool features an all-tile interior with detailed custom mosaic designs on the floor and walls. A retractable fountain bubbler along with twenty-four laminar deck jets and under-coping spray jets transform this modern Grecian style pool into an exquisite fountain that can be viewed from strategic points within the residence. At one end of the pool, a raised fire pit filled with blue fire glass, matching glass tile and mosaic patterns accent the setting. Decking consisting of travertine pavers adds an old world feel.

FEATURES

Zodiac Pool Systems, Inc.
Paramount Pool & Spa Systems

Photos courtesy of Mark Daniels.

GOLD AWARD WINNER

ALOHA POOLS PTY LTD

CATEGORY
All-Tile

PROJECT
Bayside Plunge
Portsea, Victoria, Australia
4.58 meters x 2.17 meters
(14′9″ x 7′1″)

Photos courtesy of Trevor Mein.

THE VISIONARIES

BUILDER/DESIGNER

Aloha Pools Pty Ltd
www.alohapools.com.au
03.9775.0033
Carrum Downs, Victoria, Australia
Swimming Pool & Spa Association of Victoria
Paramount Advisory Committee Enterprise

ARCHITECT

Lovell Chen Architects Pty Ltd
www.lovellchen.com.au

THE VISION

The owner of this beachside property had three main objectives for this project's vision. First and foremost, they wanted a pool that would be an aesthetic enhancement to the newly refurbished terrace. However, they wanted to avoid a design that would block the bayside view or leave no room on the patio for an outdoor entertaining area. To achieve these goals, a design was developed to give the impression of water falling over the sides of the pool. A custom blend of glass-mosaic tiles gives the water a shimmering, reflective quality.

FEATURES

Zodiac Pool Systems, Inc.
Paramount Pool & Spa Systems

SILVOR
AWARDWINNER

ALOHA POOLS PTY LTD

CATEGORY
All-Tile

PROJECT
Tuscan Living
Mornington, Victoria,
Australia
10 meters x 10 meters
(32′9″ x 32′9″)

Photos courtesy of George Kochukudiyil.

THE VISIONARIES

BUILDER

Aloha Pools Pty Ltd
www.alohapools.com.au
03.9775.0033
Carrum Downs, Victoria, Australia
Swimming Pool & Spa Association of Victoria
Paramount Advisory Committee Enterprise

DESIGNER

Greg Fell, Aloha Pools Pty Ltd

THE VISION

This design was based on a vision of enhancing the view of the nearby bay from the pool and the adjoining living areas. Large-format Italian travertine tiles were used in the interior of the pool and spa, which had to be constructed two meters aboveground. We built the pool on top of a structural water tank, providing a stable surface for construction. This also incorporated the clients' desire for water-saving solutions.

FEATURES

Zodiac Pool Systems, Inc.
Paramount Pool & Spa Systems

GOLD
AWARDWINNER

POLAR POOLS PTY LTD

CATEGORY
Geometric

PROJECT
Corlette
Corlette, New South Wales, Australia
16.7 meters (54′9″)

Photos courtesy of Andy Warren.

THE VISIONARIES

BUILDER
Norman Leth
Polar Pools Pty Ltd
www.polarpools.com.au
61.2.4981.9911
Newcastle, New South Wales, Australia
Swimming Pool & Spa Association of New South Wales

DESIGNER
Cameron Leth, Polar Pools Pty Ltd

PROJECT OWNER:
Sharpe Residence

THE VISION

The vision was to create a modern minimalist lap pool with a hint of coastal vibe. The client wanted a lap pool for exercise and a swim bowl for greater functionality. At either end of the pool are two sun lounge areas, giving the owners options depending on the location of the sun and wind. A lower level wading pool doubles as a water feature and therapeutic ice bath. Floating step pads, recessed bubblers and glass windows in the side wall add extra interest to the design.

FEATURES
Designed with Structure Studios 3-D Pool Studio
Paramount Pool & Spa Systems
Pebble Technology, Inc. Pool Finishes

GOLD
AWARDWINNER

BLUE STONE POOLS

CATEGORY
Geometric

PROJECT
West Coast Drive
Watermans Bay, Western
Australia, Australia
12 meters x 2.7 meters
(39'4" x 8'10")

Photos courtesy of Alderete Pools, Inc.

Photos courtesy of Shutterworks Photography.

THE VISIONARIES

DESIGNER/CONTRACTOR
Grant Osborne
Blue Stone Pools
www.bluestonepools.com.au
08.9249.6647
Malaga, Western Australia, Australia
Association of Pool and Spa Professionals
Master Builders Association of Australia

Brian Burke Homes
www.brianburkehomes.com.au

PROJECT OWNER:
Apted Residence

THE VISION

The vision was to create a pool that was expansive without imposing on the views. Thus the concept of a curvature pool with a glass window was designed. We created computer generated templates that replicated the radius of the home for each curve. This gave a geometrically balanced feel between the pool and home. The pool blends in creatively while being large in length. The glass window also gave depth to the width of the pool, blending harmoniously with the ocean. Interior mosaic colors match the ocean and surrounds match the beach sand.

FEATURES
Zodiac Pool Systems, Inc.

GOLD AWARD WINNER

TEXAS POOLS

CATEGORY
Geometric

PROJECT
LeBlanc
The Woodlands, Texas, USA
348 square feet

Photos courtesy of Texas Pools.

THE VISIONARIES

BUILDER/CONTRACTOR

Texas Pools
www.texaspools.com
281.367.4660
The Woodlands, Texas, USA
Association of Pool and Spa Professionals
American Society of Interior Designers
National Association of Home Builders

DESIGNER

Paul Ryan, Texas Pools

THE VISION

This project's vision was to keep the sleek lines and rich materials used in the home's architecture while providing an aesthetically pleasing and functional swimming pool. Simple lines and precise material work were crucial to the success of the design integrating properly with the home. The spa was placed on the house level and separated from the lower-level pool. Its overflow functions as the pool's primary water feature.

FEATURES

Pebble Technology, Inc. Pool Finishes
Paramount Pool & Spa Systems

GOLD AWARDWINNER

POOL ENVIRONMENTS

CATEGORY
Geometric

PROJECT
Dallas Modern
Dallas, Texas, USA
33 feet x 38 feet

Photos courtesy of Graham Hobart.

THE VISIONARIES

BUILDER

Pool Environments
www.poolenvironments.com
972.985.1576
Plano, Texas, USA
Association of Pool and Spa Professionals

DESIGNER

Randy Angell, Pool Environments

THE VISION

The vision for this pool was to reflect the architecture of the house as well as its interior design style, which called for a very clean-lined contemporary look. In addition to this, the client wanted a pool the children would appreciate now and when they are grown. All the stone work was finished in honed Leuders limestone, with no overhangs and tight joints. The decks were finished in a colored, saw-cut concrete fashioned to mimic the limestone. These selections set a subtle canvas for the aqua glass mosaic tile and the aqua interior finish to really become the stars of the show.

FEATURES

Paramount Pool & Spa Systems

SILVOR AWARDWINNER

ALOHA POOLS PTY LTD

CATEGORY
Geometric

PROJECT
Juxtaposed
Brighton, Victoria, Australia
Pool: 14 meters x 3.5 meters (45′11″ x 11′5″)
Spa: 2 meters diameter (6′6″ diameter)

Photos courtesy of George Kochukudiyil.

THE VISIONARIES

BUILDER/DESIGNER

Aloha Pools Pty Ltd
www.alohapools.com.au
03.9775.0033
Carrum Downs, Victoria, Australia
Swimming Pool & Spa Association of Victoria
Paramount Advisory Committee Enterprise

THE VISION

The vision was to create a pool and spa package that would harmonize seamlessly with the dramatic architecture of the client's home. The home has a very modern design and the pool had to keep up with this concept. Bluestone was selected for the wet-edge face to complement the modern style of the home. The pool and spa were constructed at the same level as the house so that it could be viewed as an aesthetic feature, even from inside the home. This pool makes a statement, completely free of any embellishments, relying entirely on sound design and workmanship.

FEATURES

Zodiac Pool Systems, Inc.
Paramount Pool & Spa Systems

SILVOR AWARDWINNER

TEXAS POOLS

CATEGORY
Geometric

PROJECT
Piccione
The Woodlands, Texas,
USA
323 square feet

Photos courtesy of Texas Pools.

THE VISIONARIES

BUILDER/CONTRACTOR

Texas Pools
www.texaspools.com
281.367.4660
The Woodlands, Texas, USA
Association of Pool and Spa Professionals
American Society of Interior Designers
National Association of Home Builders

DESIGNER

Mark Oberkirch, Texas Pools

THE VISION

Our vision was to create as large of a pool as possible that would also integrate features and structure from the house. The client desired plenty of pool seating and swim space, which was difficult to create as the lot was quite small. An added overhead structure was built so that the support columns rested inside the pool and on a shelf. Additionally, the same structure hides a rain curtain that flows down into the pool on the main view from the house. The spa wall functions as a walkway to access the back side of the pool area and yard.

FEATURES

Designed with Structure Studios 3-D Pool Studio
Pebble Technology, Inc. Pool Finishes

SILVOR AWARDWINNER

TEXAS POOLS

CATEGORY
Geometric

PROJECT
Creel
The Woodlands, Texas, USA
165 square feet

Photos courtesy of Texas Pools.

THE VISIONARIES

BUILDER/DESIGNER

Thom Blumenkamp
Texas Pools
www.texaspools.com
281.367.4660
The Woodlands, Texas, USA
Association of Pool and Spa Professionals
American Society of Interior Designers
National Association of Home Builders

THE VISION

The architect, homeowner and designer wanted to ensure the project looked as though everything was built with the same unified vision and that there was a seamless transition between structures. The pool had to meet strict architectural standards and integrate with the house in an extremely small space while providing an unusual number of amenities. The perimeter overflow spa, infinity edge pool and bronze cranes all add to the overall design.

FEATURES

Designed with Structure Studios 3-D Pool Studio
Paramount Pool & Spa Systems
Pebble Technology, Inc. Pool Finishes

GOLD AWARD WINNER

ALOHA POOLS PTY LTD

CATEGORY
Interior Applications

PROJECT
Indoor Sanctuary
Toorak, Victoria, Australia
21 meters x 3.5 meters
(68'10" x 11'5")

Photos courtesy of George Kochukudiyil.

THE VISIONARIES

BUILDER/DESIGNER

Aloha Pools Pty Ltd
www.alohapools.com.au
03.9775.0033
Carrum Downs, Victoria, Australia
Swimming Pool & Spa Association of Victoria
Paramount Advisory Committee Enterprise

ARCHITECT

Stephen Jolson
www.jolson.com.au

THE VISION

The vision was to provide the client with a low-maintenance pool that provided year-round usability and would be a major architectural component of the property. Since the pool was built underground, it had the added benefit of thermal insulation, making it easier to control the room and water temperature. Black tiles were used to line both the pool and columns, which rise up from the pool to provide support for the structure above. The pool design stimulates balance and harmony of the home's modern style.

FEATURES

Zodiac Pool Systems, Inc.
Paramount Pool and Spa Systems
All-tile Interior

GOLD
AWARDWINNER

MILL BERGEN POOL CENTER

CATEGORY
Interior Applications

PROJECT
Leybovich
Staten Island, New York,
USA
21 feet x 32 feet

Photos courtesy of Allen Santa Maria.

THE VISIONARIES

BUILDER/DESIGNER

Robert Blanda
Mill Bergen Pool Center
www.millbergenpools.com
718.763.5500
Brooklyn, New York, USA
Association of Pool and Spa Professionals
Northeast Spa & Pool Association

PROJECT OWNER:

Yakov Leybovich

THE VISION

This indoor pool was built on the main floor of a contemporary style one-family home. The client's vision was to have the pool viewable from anywhere in the multi-level residence. The raised beam along the entire length of the pool wall doubles as the basement wall and a water feature. Three Sheer Descents, in combination with the glass block and mosaic tile, create the finish of the wall. The decision to build the pool on the main floor was made after the house structure and foundations were completed, requiring all the excavation to be done by hand and the soil to be removed by wheel barrel.

FEATURES

Designed with Structure Studios 3-D Pool Studio
Zodiac Pool Systems, Inc.

SILVOR AWARDWINNER

SUNSET POOLS

CATEGORY
Interior Application

PROJECT
Strathfield
Strathfield, New South Wales, Australia
25 meters x 3 meters
(82′ x 9′10″)

Photos courtesy of Mitch Cammeron Photography.

THE VISIONARIES

BUILDER
Sunset Pools
www.sunsetpools.com.au
1300.000.412
North Ryde, New South Wales, Australia
Association of Pool and Spa Professionals
Swimming Pool & Spa Association of Australia
Master Builders Association

ARCHITECT
Supersoma Architects

CONTRACTOR
Kanaan Kanaan
Komplete Constructions Pty Ltd
www.kompleteconstruction.com.au

PROJECT OWNER:
Quin On

THE VISION

The vision was to create an environment for year-round enjoyment and comfort. This project required the most stringent construction program, forcing the pool to be built at the same time as the designer residence. The end result is an outstanding indoor lap pool with extraordinary touches, such as fully-tiled glass mosaics applied with epoxy grouting and roll over weir so the kids can slide in and out of the spa.

GOLD AWARDWINNER

TRUE BLUE SWIMMING POOLS

CATEGORY
Vinyl Lined

PROJECT
Lagoon with Grotto
Centerport, New York, USA
25 feet x 38 feet

Photos courtesy of True Blue Swimming Pools.

THE VISIONARIES

BUILDER
Michael Truehart
True Blue Swimming Pools
www.trueblueswimmingpools.com
631.757.7665
Dix Hills, New York, USA
Association of Pool and Spa Professionals

DESIGNER
Crystal Meadows, Inc.
www.crystalmeadowsinc.com

THE VISION

Rising sixty feet over the harbor, this natural freeform pool includes a true grotto with benches and an overhead waterfall. All of the surrounding amenities were chosen to evoke the vision of a Caribbean-style lagoon. Adding to the resort feel is a built-in bar at pool level, as well as a raised barbeque area convenient to both the pool and house. To complete the effect, a brown sandstone vinyl liner that reacts with the water was utilized to create a beautiful turquoise color.

FEATURES
Zodiac Pool Systems, Inc.

GOLD AWARD WINNER

POOL ENVIRONMENTS

CATEGORY
Renovation

PROJECT
Modern Renovation
Dallas, Texas, USA
23 feet x 41 feet

THE VISIONARIES

BUILDER
Pool Environments
www.poolenvironments.com
972.985.1576
Plano, Texas, USA
Association of Pool and Spa Professionals

DESIGNER
Randy Angell, Pool Environments

THE VISION

The new homeowners had no desire to "play it safe" with the vision of this renovation. We utilized the simple, straight lines of the existing pool to lay out a multi-level outdoor living space with a sun lounge area and a cooking and dining area. A smooth-finished colored concrete with a saw-cut score pattern took the place of the outdated seeded aggregate decking. The pool was framed with a chartreuse stucco wall on one side and stucco in charcoal grey on the other. The "wow factor" was created with a striking fireplace that features a three-foot cantilevered mantle.

Before.

Photos courtesy of Graham Hobart, Micah Nunley.

SILVOR
AWARDWINNER

VENEZOLANA DE PISCINAS I, C.A.

CATEGORY
Renovation

PROJECT
Perez
El Solar, Venezuela, South America
780 square feet

Photos courtesy of Pierre Tairous.

Before.

THE VISIONARIES

BUILDER/DESIGNER/CONTRACTOR

Edwin Vives
Venezolana de Piscinas I, C.A.
www.venezolanadepiscinas.com
58.414.3593754
Valencia, Venezuela, South America

PROJECT OWNER:

Roviro Perez

THE VISION

This project was an extreme makeover of what was once a small pool in an open field. The vision was to turn the courtyard area into the new center of attention for the house. A large deck surrounds the pool for social gatherings. The deck lighting contrasts with the LED pool lights, offering a strange mix that is very pleasing to the eye.

FEATURES

Designed with Structure Studios 3-D Pool Studio
All-tile Interior

SILVOR AWARDWINNER

NATURAL WATER ENVIRONMENTS

CATEGORY
Renovation

PROJECT
Lyons Renovation
Coppell, Texas, USA
22,000 gallons

Before.

Photos courtesy of Craig Cameron.

THE VISIONARIES

BUILDER/DESIGNER

Craig Cameron
Natural Water Environments
www.natural-water-env.com
817.355.0417
Dallas, Texas, USA
Association of Pool and Spa Professionals

LANDSCAPER:

Grow It Designs
www.growitlanddesigns.com

PROJECT OWNER:

Selena and Shawn Lyons

THE VISION

The clients love to entertain and had a vision of transforming their drab backyard into a visual and functional entertainment oasis. The conversion of the deck level spa into a spectacular water feature was the real focal point. We designed a dramatic combination of features that included bubblers, Sheer Descents, LED colored illumination lights and a six-foot crescent-shaped fire pit, which also serves as an additional seating area. The resulting backyard transformation is dramatic during the day but even more spectacular at night.

FEATURES

Paramount Pool & Spa Systems

GOLD AWARD WINNER

PATIO POOLS & SPAS

CATEGORY
Spa
PROJECT
Wood
Tucson, Arizona, USA
11 feet x 8 feet

Photos courtesy of Patio Pools & Spas.

THE VISIONARIES

BUILDER
Patio Pools & Spas
www.patiopoolsaz.com
520.886.1211
Tucson, Arizona, USA
Association of Pool and Spa Professionals

DESIGNER
Michael Cojanis, Patio Pools & Spas

THE VISION

Constructed of natural stone, this desert oasis was made to replicate an artesian spring. The vision was to use only local materials and make the area look as natural as possible, yet still have the comforts of a modern-day spa. Rocks were painstakingly collected from around the property and assembled on site. Spa jets were hidden between rocks that plunged below the waterline and down to the bench. Fittings, such as the skimmer throat and deck lids, were all constructed from rock and set to disappear into the landscape.

FEATURES
Pebble Technology, Inc. Pool Finishes

GOLD AWARD WINNER

AQUA BLUE POOLS

CATEGORY
Spa

PROJECT
Michael's Residence
Lake Sherwood, California, USA
8 feet x 12 feet

Photo courtesy of Aqua Blue Pools.

THE VISIONARIES

BUILDER/CONTRACTOR
Aqua Blue Pools
www.aquabluecreations.com
805.499.0972
Newbury Park, California, USA
Association of Pool and Spa Professionals

ARCHITECT/DESIGNER
James Dean Design
www.jamesdeandesign.com

THE VISION

The vision was to create a spa that would complement the lake below as well as the design of the home. The spa extends over the top of the house, making it necessary to provide deepened footings along the outer edge of the spa's excavation. Features of this rooftop application include a Pebble Sheen finish and travertine decking.

FEATURES
Zodiac Pool Systems, Inc.
Pebble Technology, Inc. Pool Finishes

GOLD AWARD WINNER

ALDERETE POOLS, INC.

CATEGORY
Spa

PROJECT
Green
Orange County, California, USA
8 feet x 12 feet

Photos courtesy of Alderete Pools, Inc.

THE VISIONARIES

BUILDER/DESIGNER/CONTRACTOR
Alderete Pools, Inc.
www.alderetepools.com
800.492.7289
San Clemente, California, USA
Association of Pool and Spa Professionals

THE VISION

The vision was to create a natural setting emphasizing a tropical jungle theme. The spa was constructed entirely of man-made sculptured boulders and stone decking. Features include three fire elements and two waterfalls, enhancing the exotic lagoon environment. A grotto with a seating area sits behind the large waterfall while the surrounding trough gives the spa a zero-edge feature.

FEATURES
Paramount Pool & Spa Systems
Pebble Technology, Inc. Pool Finishes

SILVOR AWARDWINNER

HYDROSCAPES LLC

CATEGORY
Spa

PROJECT
Schuler
Paradise Valley, Arizona, USA
8 feet x 11 feet

Photos courtesy of Scott Sandler.

THE VISIONARIES

BUILDER/DESIGNER/CONTRACTOR
Roger Soares II
Hydroscapes LLC
www.hydroscapes.com
480.837.6844
Scottsdale, Arizona, USA
Society of Watershape Designers

THE VISION

This spa was created with the vision of a private retreat - an area to sit and enjoy in the courtyard. As a gift for the wife, the client wanted the design to fit with the style of the home and the water to be as blue as the waters of Bermuda. This color was achieved by using a custom blend of Sicis glass for the all-tile interior. Custom copper cannon spillways and copper gas lamps were installed to match those on the house.

FEATURES
All-tile Interior

SILVOR AWARDWINNER

ALDERETE POOLS, INC.

CATEGORY
Spa

PROJECT
Tien
Orange County, California, USA
8 feet x 8 feet

Photos courtesy of Alderete Pools, Inc.

THE VISIONARIES

BUILDER/DESIGNER/CONTRACTOR
Alderete Pools, Inc.
www.alderetepools.com
800.492.7289
San Clemente, California, USA
Association of Pool and Spa Professionals

THE VISION

This spa was designed to fit within an elegant country club theme. That vision is enhanced by the spa's raised three-sided infinity edge, which was built with custom colored concrete coping. A unique blue granite surface was hand-cut and applied to the spa seating area along with the sloped top and side walls. The spa is surrounded by two professional regulation putting greens.

FEATURES
Paramount Pool & Spa Systems

GOLD AWARD WINNER

TEXAS POOLS

CATEGORY
Water Feature

PROJECT
Hekker
The Woodlands, Texas, USA
62 square feet

Photos courtesy of Texas Pools.

THE VISIONARIES

BUILDER/CONTRACTOR

Texas Pools
www.texaspools.com
281.367.4660
The Woodlands, Texas, USA
Association of Pool and Spa Professionals
American Society of Interior Designers
National Association of Home Builders

DESIGNER

Thom Blumenkamp, Texas Pools

THE VISION

The vision was to provide an old world look that would not interfere with the flow of the space while providing an aesthetic feature and functional retreat. The waterwall is integrated into the property's barrier structure, surrounding the entire lot. The trickling sound of water gives a light audible ambiance, allowing for a soothing sound without overpowering a conversation. The height of the water feature's catch basin provides informal seating for the fire pit, which is nestled in front of the fountain.

FEATURES

Designed with Structure Studios 3-D Pool Studio
Pebble Technology, Inc. Pool Finishes

SILVOR AWARDWINNER

MAC LANDSCAPING INC.

CATEGORY
Water Feature

PROJECT
Ruiz Residence
Las Vegas, Nevada, USA

Photos courtesy of Mary Vail, OSG Publicist.

THE VISIONARIES

BUILDER/DESIGNER
Mike Newman
MAC Landscaping Inc.
www.maclandscape.com
702.221.8049
Las Vegas, Nevada, USA

THE VISION

The vision was to create a complete outdoor space incorporating water and fire as a stimulus. A multi-level, dual water feature brook was crafted with the use of natural stone boulders and pebbles. At one end, water flows from an elevated curved canal with peephole cutouts, adding visual intrigue as well as enhancing the audible effects of the water. Floating slate step pads allow one to cross the brook to a secluded sitting area, a secondary water feature or the large entertainment area. A variety of textures and structures including rock-filled gabion columns, basalt columns, along with LED lighting, a fire pit, and lush softscape create a peaceful setting for day or night.

GOLD AWARD WINNER

ALOHA POOLS PTY LTD

CATEGORY
Glass Panels

PROJECT
Private Aquarium
Albert Park, Victoria, Australia
5.1 meters x 1.9 meters
(16′8″ x 6′2″)

Photos courtesy of George Kochukudiyil.

THE VISIONARIES

BUILDER/DESIGNER
Aloha Pools Pty Ltd
www.alohapools.com.au
03.9775.0033
Carrum Downs, Victoria, Australia
Swimming Pool & Spa Association of Victoria
Paramount Advisory Committee Enterprise

ARCHITECT
Nicholas Murray Architects
www.nma.net.au

THE VISION

The client's vision was for the pool to act as an aesthetic feature even when it wasn't in use. The incorporation of glass panels in the side of the concrete shell contributes to this vision by allowing the pool to serve as a water feature not only in the traditional outdoor sense, but also from within the home. The interior of the pool also serves as a unique feature, with its use of shimmering Italian glass mosaic tiles.

FEATURES
Zodiac Pool Systems, Inc.
Paramount Pool & Spa Systems

GOLD AWARD WINNER

SPRING CREEK POOL & SPA, INC.

CATEGORY
Structure Studios: Pool Studio 3-D & Infinity Edge

PROJECT
Baker
Granite Bay, California, USA
30,000 square feet

Structure Studios 3-D image.

Photos courtesy of Spring Creek Pool & Spa, Inc.

THE VISIONARIES

BUILDER

Spring Creek Pool & Spa, Inc.
www.springcreekpools.com
209.599.5502
Ripon, California, USA
Association of Pool and Spa Professionals

STRUCTURE STUDIOS 3-D DESIGNER

Matt Tankersley, Spring Creek Pool & Spa

POOL DESIGNER/CONTRACTOR

Eddie Erdelatz, Spring Creek Pool & Spa, Inc.

COLLABORATOR:

Greg Wheatley, Spring Creek Pool & Spa, Inc.

PROJECT OWNER:

Baker Residence

THE VISION

The concept was to make two styles of pool merge seamlessly within one project. Designing the multiple water elements, split level pools and isolated spa would have been a challenge to conceive visually without the assistance of the Pool Studio 3D application. The program allowed for a 360-degree viewing from any elevation on the property, giving the design team and the client a true perspective of the elaborate multi-dimensional project.

The most notable feature of the project is the upper pool's eighteen-foot infinity edge, which cantilevers over the lower pool. The upper pool also has two copper sheer-style water features. The lower pool is more playful and boasts a swim-up bar, twelve-foot infinity edge, three custom-fabricated fire features, masonry detail, and glass tile.

FEATURES

Designed with Structure Studios 3-D Pool Studio

BRONZE AWARD WINNER

DISTINGUISHED POOLS, INC.

CATEGORY
Structure Studios:
Pool Studio
3-D & Fire

PROJECT
Eclectic Charm
Carlsbad, California, USA
25 feet x 55 feet

A Structure Studio 3-D image.

Photos courtesy of Darren Edwards.

THE VISIONARIES

BUILDER/DESIGNER/CONTRACTOR

Dan Ramos
Distinguished Pools
www.distinguishedpools.com
858.204.1532
Poway, California, USA
Association of Pool and Spa Professionals

THE VISION

The vision was to add a creative statement to an existing pool without shouting. Utilizing the Pool Studio 3-D application, we illustrated to the homeowner how the raised fire elements would add a striking dimension to the pool. Three custom-made, copper fire bowls with water spouts are elevated on handcrafted travertine-tiled pedestals. The pool's existing all-tile interior was already a perfect match for the unique architecture of the home. Preserving it during the reconstruction was a major challenge but proved well worth it given the final result.

FEATURES

Designed with Structure Studios 3-D Pool Studio
Zodiac Pool Systems, Inc.

GOLD AWARDWINNER

POOL ENVIRONMENTS

CATEGORY
Marine Habitat

PROJECT
Koi
Fort Worth, Texas, USA
5 feet x 50 feet

Photos courtesy of Graham Hobart.

THE VISIONARIES

BUILDER
Pool Environments
www.poolenvironments.com
972.985.1576
Plano, Texas, USA
Association of Pool and Spa Professionals

DESIGNER/ARCHITECT
Bill Bibb, Archiverde Landscape Architecture,
www.archiverde-us.com
Turner Boaz Architecture, www.turnerboaz.com

THE VISION

The vision was to show the client's eclectic taste through a series of five unique water features on the property. The project includes a koi pond, water garden and waterwall that acts as a "moat" to the entrance of the residence. Thick blocks of native Texas limestone create floating bridges for visitors to access the home. It was imperative that the project not relate to its environment as much as define it. Each body of water makes its own individual statement regarding its space.

FEATURES
Zodiac Pool Systems, Inc.

SILVOR AWARDWINNER

JORGE GRAÇA COSTA - ARCHITECT

CATEGORY
Green Applications

PROJECT
U House
Ericeira, Portugal
30 square meters
(98 sq. feet, 5")

Photos courtesy of FG+SG.

THE VISIONARIES

ARCHITECT

Jorge Graça Costa - Architect
00351.966.539.539
00351.214.427.702
Oeiras, Portugal

BUILDER

Carré Bleu Ericeira

CONTRACTOR/PROJECT OWNER:

José Gregório

THE VISION

The client's U-shaped house gives the pool a comfortable level of privacy and thermal comfort, sheltering it from street views and prevailing winds. The vision was to enhance this comfort with numerous "green" applications. The pool's sustainable features include its micro-climate environment created by the patio, LED illumination, pool water without chemical treatment, and rainwater harvesting (collected in a preexisting well) for irrigation. The pool's success in harmonizing design, functionality and sustainability is augmented by its livability and considerable savings in water consumption and energy use.

GOLD AWARD WINNER

COVERTECH LLC

CATEGORY
Technology

PROJECT
SCHSH Long Island
Long Island, New York, USA
19 feet x 43 feet

Photos courtesy of Covertech LLC.

THE VISIONARIES

INVENTOR/DESIGNER

Torsten Heincke
Covertech LLC
www.poolcovertech.com
631.287.9495
Southampton, New York, USA
Association of Pool and Spa Professionals

ARCHITECT

Mark Matthews, Architect
www.matthewsarchitect.com

POOL BUILDER

Imperial Gunite
www.imperialgunite.com

THE VISION

This design was inspired by a vision of providing the client with a setting similar to a private beach. Construction was a challenge as there was a fifteen-foot drop into the dunes area. In a three-day work process, the drop was filled in with sand to provide the proper elevation from the dunes and offer the perfect oceanfront view. The pool features a custom Covertech pool cover.

BRONZE
AWARDWINNER

COVERTECH LLC

CATEGORY
Technology

PROJECT
EHRi Long Island
Long Island, New York, USA
18 feet x 65 feet

Photos courtesy of Covertech LLC

THE VISIONARIES

INVENTOR/DESIGNER
Torsten Heincke
Covertech LLC
www.poolcovertech.com
631.287.9495
Southampton, New York, USA
Association of Pool and Spa Professionals

ARCHITECT
Marmol Radziner
www.marmol-radziner.com

POOL BUILDER
Pristine Pools
www.swimpristinepools.com

THE VISION

The vision was to provide energy efficiency and address safety concerns with a pool cover. Both the pool and spa were fitted with custom automatic rigid-slated covers allowing for eighty percent energy efficiency to maintain water temperature for year-round enjoyment. The pool features dual vanishing edges and is elevated 25 feet above ground to overlook the back of the property, which was built into a mountain slope.

BRONZE AWARDWINNER

COVERTECH LLC

CATEGORY
Technology

PROJECT
ANEH Long Island
Long Island, New York, USA
20 feet x 60 feet

Photos courtesy of Covertech LLC.

THE VISIONARIES

INVENTOR/DESIGNER

Torsten Heincke
Covertech LLC
www.poolcovertech.com
631.287.9495
Southampton, New York, USA
Association of Pool and Spa Professionals

POOL BUILDER

Pristine Pools
www.swimpristinepools.com

THE VISION

The vision was to design a cover for multiple purposes: a safety barrier, protection from the weather elements, and energy efficiency – without sacrificing the pool's visual appeal. The pool features a fully-automated polycarbonate rigid-slated cover that allows night illumination for background ambience. Because it floats directly on the water, the pool cover allows eighty percent energy efficiency for heating, as well as minimizing maintenance, water evaporation and chemical use.

BRONZE AWARDWINNER

COVERTECH LLC

CATEGORY
Technology

PROJECT
EH Long Island
Long Island, New York, USA
18 feet x 65 feet

Photos courtesy of Covertech LLC.

THE VISIONARIES

INVENTOR/DESIGNER
Torsten Heincke
Covertech LLC
www.poolcovertech.com
631.287.9495
Southampton, New York, USA
Association of Pool and Spa Professionals

ARCHITECT
Edmund Hollander Landscape Architect Design P.C.
www.hollanderdesign.com

CONTRACTOR
Tortorella Pools
www.tortorella.com

THE VISION

The vision was to provide security with a pool cover that would not sacrifice any aesthetics. This was especially important at night time, when the pool needed to be covered but look as if it was open with the lights shining through. The rigid-slated automatic pool cover was precision cut to fit the geometric design and allows night illumination when the cover is closed, creating a sleek and inconspicuous design.

GOLD AWARD WINNER

POOL ENVIRONMENTS

CATEGORY
Art

PROJECT
Mermaid
Dallas, Texas, USA
997 square feet

Photos courtesy of Graham Hobart.

THE VISIONARIES

BUILDER
Pool Environments
www.poolenvironments.com
972.985.1576
Plano, Texas, USA
Association of Pool and Spa Professionals

DESIGNER
Randy Angell
Pool Environments

THE VISION

The vision was to create a unique artistic element that would accent the natural pond and waterfall designs. We wanted everything to appear as though one had just stumbled upon an escape in the woods. The bronze mermaid statue is positioned in a prominent axis of view from the residence and placed in an all-glass tile fountain basin with cannon jets, LED lights and a fog system. The fountain ties to the pool via a rambling creek.

FEATURES
Zodiac Pool Systems, Inc.
Paramount Pool & Spa Systems

GOLD AWARD WINNER

POOL ENVIRONMENTS

CATEGORY
Fire

PROJECT
Sizzle
Highland Park, Texas, USA
11 feet x 30 feet

Photos courtesy of Graham Hobart.

THE VISIONARIES

BUILDER

Pool Environments
www.poolenvironments.com
972.985.1576
Plano, Texas, USA
Association of Pool and Spa Professionals

DESIGNER

Randy Angell, Pool Environments

THE VISION

The project began by walking through the remodeled home with the client. Their vision was to complete the property with a modern backyard that was energized yet relaxing. A custom fire feature follows the base of the curved stucco wall, which is adorned with bamboo, for fourteen feet and disappears behind a grey stucco accent wall. The opening in the accent wall has a rain curtain, suggesting an intermingling of fire and water.

FEATURES

Zodiac Pool Systems, Inc.

GOLD AWARDWINNER

STONECREST POOLS

CATEGORY
Fire

PROJECT
Courtyard Spa
Dallas, Texas, USA
15 feet x 12 feet

Photos courtesy of Sean Gallagher.

THE VISIONARIES

BUILDER/CONTRACTOR

StoneCrest Pools
www.stonecrestpools.com
817.988.2941
Keller, Texas, USA
Association of Pool and Spa Professionals
Genesis3 Gold Member

DESIGNER

Doug Johnston, StoneCrest Pools

THE VISION

The vision was to create a private retreat courtyard outside the master bedroom for relaxation and release from everyday stress. The result was an oversized arched waterwall with a long, narrow curved fire element creating a mesmerizing focal point just off the raised perimeter overflow all-tile spa. The spa features custom designed lounges inside to fit the client's dimensions.

FEATURES

Designed with Structure Studios 3-D Pool Studio

GOLD AWARD WINNER

STONECREST POOLS

CATEGORY
Personal Waterpark

PROJECT
Private Ranch in Texas Play Park
Dallas, Texas, USA
365 feet x 9 feet

Photos courtesy of Sean Gallagher.

THE VISIONARIES

BUILDER/CONTRACTOR

StoneCrest Pools
www.stonecrestpools.com
817.988.2941
Keller, Texas, USA
Association of Pool and Spa Professionals
Genesis3 Gold Member

DESIGNER

Doug Johnston, StoneCrest Pools

THE VISION

This project's vision was to build a personal, one-of-a-kind waterpark for a residential home. The centerpiece of the design is the lazy river, which was created with the client's grandchildren in mind. The waterpark features eighteen spray-park toys – one for each grandchild – five river flow pumps for multiple river speeds, twelve fire torches, a sound system, Pebble Fina finish, glass waterline tile, four waterfalls and four Sheer Descents on two stone bridges. The lazy river and spray park can all be controlled via iPhone.

FEATURES

Designed with Structure Studios 3-D Pool Studio
Pebble Technology, Inc. Pool Finishes

Section Two

COMMERCIAL AQUATEKTURE

GOLD AWARDWINNER

ALOHA POOLS PTY LTD

CATEGORY
Interior Application

PROJECT
Inner City
Melbourne, Victoria, Australia
Lap pool: 25 meters x 4 meters (82′ x 13′1″)
Children's pool: 4 meters x 3 meters (13′1″ x 9′10″)
Spa: 4.3 meters x 3.3 meters (14′1″ x 10′9″)

Photos courtesy of Michael Kai.

THE VISIONARIES

BUILDER
Aloha Pools Pty Ltd
www.alohapools.com.au
03.9775.0033
Carrum Downs, Victoria, Australia
Swimming Pool & Spa Association of Victoria
Paramount Advisory Committee Enterprise

ARCHITECT
Preston Lane Architects
www.prestonlanearchitects.com.au

DESIGNER
SJB Interiors
www.sjb.com.au

CONTRACTOR
Easton Builders
www.eastonbuilders.com.au

THE VISION

This project was completed as part of the refurbishment of a luxurious, high-end apartment building on St. Kilda Road in Melbourne. The vision was to rejuvenate the pools and spa in a way that would be harmonious with the high-quality finishes used for the surrounding area. The swimming pool, spa and children's pool all had to be stripped back to their structural shell, remodeled and then have new finishes applied.

FEATURES
All-tile Interior

SILVOR AWARD WINNER

PATIO POOLS & SPAS

CATEGORY
Resort Pool

PROJECT
Casino Del Sol
Tucson, Arizona, USA
147,000 gallons

Photos courtesy of Patio Pools & Spas.

THE VISIONARIES

BUILDER
Patio Pools & Spas
www.patiopoolsaz.com
520.886.1211
Tucson, Arizona, USA
Association of Pool and Spa Professionals

ARCHITECT
Leo A. Daly Architects
www.leoadaly.com

CONTRACTOR
McCarthy Construction
www.mccarthy.com

PROJECT OWNER:
Casino Del Sol

THE VISION

Local tribal leadership in collaboration with the architect and Patio Pools & Spas set forth a vision of Old World Spanish charm meets contemporary living. The swimming pool and spa area is framed by cabanas, a poolside bar and a roman aqueduct. These features accommodate a variety of ages, diverse interests and aesthetic values. This project required two miles of plumbing and the creation of a program to synchronize the waterfeatures to 'dance' to the rhythm of music.

FEATURES
Designed with Structure Studios 3-D Pool Studio
Pebble Technology, Inc. Pool Finishes

SILVOR
AWARDWINNER

SPRING CREEK POOL & SPA, INC.

CATEGORY
Resort Spa

PROJECT
Wine and Roses
Lodi, California, USA
Two spas: 8 feet diameter each

Photos courtesy of Spring Creek Pool & Spa, Inc.

THE VISIONARIES

BUILDER
Spring Creek Pool & Spa, Inc.
www.springcreekpools.com
209.599.5502
Ripon, California, USA
Association of Pool and Spa Professionals

DESIGNER/CONTRACTOR
Eddie Erdelatz, Spring Creek Pool & Spa, Inc.

COLLABORATOR:
Greg Wheatley, Spring Creek Pool & Spa, Inc.

PROJECT OWNER:
Russ Munson

THE VISION

The vision was to maintain the "early California" architectural style of the resort. Natural, rustic materials were used to create the appearance. Two dipping pools are fed by a natural spring. Heated water is sent to the spas through a thirty-foot-long rock bed stream waterfall. Other features include hand-fabricated stone coping and granite tile with sandblasted and hand-painted depth markers. Each spa is kept at different temperatures for spa therapy treatments.

FEATURES
Zodiac Pool Systems, Inc.
Pebble Technology, Inc. Pool Finishes

Section Three

THE GAVA TEAM

THE JUDGES

A panel of judges comprising of elite professionals from several disciplines reviewed and ranked the finalists. All entries were identified by a number; entrant, builder, designer, and owner names were kept anonymous. Entries were judged on their aesthetic beauty, as well as how each exemplifies the objectives of the project: designs exhibiting original and diverse concepts that demonstrate respect for environmental, cultural, philosophical and/or historical components.

KASSIE SMITH

Founder/President
Kassie Smith Lifestyle Group
Las Vegas, Nevada, USA
www.kassiesmithlifestylegroup.com

Kassie Smith has gained the reputation of a true leader and force in the interior design and architecture industry with a career that has spanned more than two decades.

Her progression from an interior designer to becoming involved in all levels of project development has led to the formation of her current company, Kassie Smith Lifestyle Group. For the last decade Smith has served a vital role on mega project teams throughout the West Coast. Clients include: City Center Residential (Mandarin Oriental & Veer Towers), Intrawest, Centex Destination Properties, Ritz Carlton, Waldorf Astoria, PGA West, and Master Developer of Lake Las Vegas Resort. Smith supplied a turnkey of services to developers of multi-million dollar luxury destination resort properties and resort golf and spa communities. She has been responsible for design conceptualization, planning, branding, project management, product-sourcing, supplying and procuring of all Furniture, Fixtures & Equipment (FF&E).

Smith and her seasoned team have received several awards along with a solid reputation for delivering turnkey furniture packages to the developers for the luxury vacation second home market. Because of her diverse knowledge and skill, Smith works as an overall project consultant and has gained a reputation with her developers for delivering a "five star experience," embracing every aspect of the project and always staying well within budget. In the government sector, Smith held a four-year consulting contract with the City of Henderson, where she specified, purchased and procured FF&E for their large scale projects including the 250,000 sq. ft. city hall expansion development. This project required her to manage a $6 million budget.

To expand her brand further, she has launched private label hospitality furniture collections and now manufactures sixty percent of the furniture she specifies on projects. Smith is authoring her first book on "Destination Design" and is an industry leader and keynote speaker.

NEBIYOU TEKLE, LEED AP, BPI, RESNET

Dakem & Associates, LLC
Las Vegas, Nevada, USA

An accomplished architect with over a decade of experience, Nebiyou Tekle specializes in Leadership in Energy and Environmental Design (LEED).

Born in Addis Ababa, Ethiopia, Tekle moved to the United States in 1988 with his family. He sought a career in architecture after becoming intrigued by intricate, symbolic and exquisite designs of sacred places such as churches, synagogues, and mosques.

Tekle studied at Virginia Tech where he earned both a bachelor's and master's degree in architecture with a concentration in industrial design. His work and scholastic experience spans the globe from design and field management with Michael Ryan Architects, to the research, design, and proposal of a 41-story office tower for the 2008 Beijing Olympic Games in conjunction with the China Institute of Building and as a ceramic studio assistant and tutor at Virginia Tech. His immersion classes included studies at the Artigas

Ceramic Foundation in Barcelona, Spain and at The Shakers Village in Mercer, Kentucky.

In 2005, Tekle moved to Las Vegas, Nevada. He has worked with notable firms including the Friedmutter Group, and JMA Architects, where he worked on various projects ranging from multi-tower high-rise condominiums, to healthcare, hospitality and public works. Tekle is currently Project Manager for Dakem & Associates, LLC where he is responsible for Commercial & Residential Building Energy Assessment and performing Building Energy Audits using ASHRAE & US ACE protocols.

Training in diverse disciplines has allowed Tekle to conceive and evaluate projects from numerous platforms. A multi-faceted architect-artist, Tekle works in a variety of mediums including: pottery, etching, drafting, carpentry, landscaping, metalwork, plasterwork, photography, slip casting, graphic design and print, book construction, shoe and bag construction and silk screening.

An award-winning designer, Tekle has received accolades for: Emerging Professional Young Architect Forum logo design AIA Las Vegas – 1st Place Prize; his Monosole design – Robert Reuter Prize, 1st Place; and Honorable Mention for Firedisk in the Solar House Competition. He was also part of the design team for One Queensridge Place that garnered a GAVA award in 2010.

A multi-linguist, Tekle speaks Amharic, Arabic, English, and French.

JENNIFER MARGISON
Landscape Design Architect
Attanasio Landscape Architecture
www.ala-lv.com
Las Vegas, Nevada, USA

Jennifer Margison has cultivated her design career at Attanasio Landscape Architecture in Las Vegas where she enjoys the excitement of creating dynamic landscapes in the hospitality and resort industry along with the traditional design projects in the public and private sectors.

Ms. Margison grew up in Las Vegas, Nevada, where her family founded a civil engineering and land surveying company. After spending some time in Southern California working in the travel industry and studying marine biology, she returned to her hometown of Las Vegas, Nevada to become the Director of Operations for Kraemer Engineering Co., Inc., the family business, where she oversaw all aspects of business management.

Ms. Margison earned a Bachelor of Landscape Architecture degree from the University of Nevada- Las Vegas in 2005. During her studies she received the School of Fine Arts Academic Honors Award, numerous scholarship awards, and was inducted into the Sigma Lambda Alpha National Honor Society. In 2003, she gained national recognition when she won first place in the American Society of Landscape Architects competition, Undergraduate Individual Research Award for her project, "Station Area Redevelopment for Rural Communities through Comparative Impacts Analysis."

Ms. Margison's talents include experience in a wide range of assignments from parks and civic, to resort/casino, high-rise, commercial and residential. As a member of the award winning team at Attanasio Landscape Architecture, she has collaborated on such notable projects as: The Neon Boneyard Park, Boulder Plaza, Hidden Falls Park, Las Vegas Springs Preserve, Caesars Palace-Garden of the Gods, and Echelon-Streetscape Enhancements, to name a few. Margison's collaboration on the Meyer's project resulted in GAVA Gold in 2009.

She brings project design and extensive plant material knowledge to the projects and additionally has over twenty years of business experience, with progressive responsibilities in management, sales/marketing, and customer service. These skills have led her to more effectively provide valuable and responsive design services to the landscape architecture field.

THE SPONSERS

STRUCTURE STUDIOS – PRESENTING SPONSOR

www.structurestudios.com

Structure Studios is a software development company specializing in 3D visualization with groundbreaking products like Pool Studio Pool Design Software, an innovative computer-based program that allows designers to transform 2D concept to 3D virtual tours. Pool Studio transforms an ordinary, flat design into an interactive, photorealistic, 3D environment for consumers to explore: walk around, fly up in the air and view the backyard from any point or angle. With international headquarters based in Las Vegas, Nevada, Structure Studios spans the globe with thousands of pool builders, designers, and salespeople actively using the program in fifteen countries including the US, Australia, Mexico, and the United Arab Emirates.

ZODIAC – PLATINUM SPONSOR

Zodiac Pool Systems, Inc., a subsidiary of Zodiac Marine & Pool and a Carlyle Group portfolio company, is a world leader in swimming pool and spa products. The company's comprehensive product lines are marketed under the leading brand names of Baracuda®, Jandy®, Nature2®, Polaris® and Cover Pools®. Zodiac Pool Systems is the leading provider of premium, innovative pool and spa products and is committed to designing and producing the most energy efficient, earth friendly pool products and systems available. To learn more about Zodiac Pool Systems, visit www.zodiacpoolsystems.com or call 800-822-7933.

PARAMOUNT POOL & SPA SYSTEMS – GOLD SPONSOR

www.1paramount.com

Paramount Pool and Spa Systems is the World's #1 In-Floor Cleaning Systems company with a history of innovation since 1964. An American manufacturer with a pool building heritage, located in Chandler, Arizona, Paramount also offers six premier in-floor cleaning systems, Virginia Graeme Baker 2008 Compliant safety drains, Clear O3 water purification systems, JetPaks for the ultimate in-ground spa therapy, water features and many other fine products.

PEBBLE TECHNOLOGY, INC. – GOLD SPONSOR

Pebble Technology, Inc. was the first to patent the process for durable, naturally beautiful pebble pool finishes in the United States over two decades ago. Since that time, its unique formulas have been the industry standard for excellence. Pebble Tec®, Pebble Sheen® and Pebble Fina® brand pool finishes are only installed by licensed, trained experts and are backed by a company with a solid reputation for customer service. Experience the natural, refined, and old world elegance offered by Pebble Technology, Inc. Superior Quality Pool Finishes at www.pebbletec.com or call 800.937.5058.

2012 INSPIRE AWARD HONOREE

Inspire Award, recognizing individuals who inspire greatness in others through their unselfish devotion, creativity and passion in the field of AquaTekture.

VANCE GILLETTE

Vice President of Business Development
Zodiac

Vance Gillette has been in the swimming pool industry for forty-five years. He has traveled extensively throughout the United States, Europe, Canada and Australia representing such industry leaders as Jandy Products, Teledyne Laars, and now as the Vice President of Business Development for Zodiac Pool Systems.

Over the last twenty-five years, Gillette has been known as the most passionate, outspoken advocate for promoting the POSITIVE pool experience. He has written many articles and given speeches regarding the need for industry promotion to the consumer. Gillette has been a featured speaker at numerous industry trade association conferences on the tremendous value and enjoyment of pool and spa ownership.

Since 1990, his articles and commentaries have appeared in *Pool and Spa Marketing* (Canada), *Pool and Spa News*, *Swimming Pool Magazine* (England), *Swimming Pool Age* (Australia), *Service Industry News*, *Aqua Magazine*, and *WaterShapes*.

Vance truly believes, "It's all about the experience. That's our business, fulfilling our clients' desire for the overall backyard entertainment experience. That's why we should be the world's most vocal proponents of the excitement and unabashed joy of owning a great outdoor environment."

A highly respected marketing professional, Gillette keeps abreast of the latest trends in both traditional and merging media. One can easily connect with this marketing master through any number of social media outlets, including Facebook, twitter, pinterest, and LinkedIn, where he shares notable information and stunning images of water design elements.

He is affiliated with the Sales Marketing Executive Association and has completed the American Management Association Senior Executive Management course. Gillette currently serves on Association of Pool and Spa Professional (APSP) Builders Council and the SPEC Board of Governors.

THREE V ENTERPRISES

Three V Enterprises, a Las Vegas based corporation, is devoted to developing platforms to honor, educate and inspire architects, designers, builders, manufactures, and developers worldwide.

BOARD OF DIRECTORS

JOSEPH M. VASSALLO, CBP
Co-Founder, Three V Enterprises
President, Paragon Pools
Las Vegas, Nevada, USA
www.paragonpoolslv.com

Author, designer, entrepreneur, and innovator, Joseph Vassallo's talents extend well beyond his award winning firm, Paragon Pools of Las Vegas, Nevada, benefiting the industry and consumers across the globe.

Founder and president of a custom in-ground, commercial and residential construction company, Vassallo's innovative design concepts and business acumen have been celebrated in a multitude of arenas; from consumer and business publications, to electronic media and on the web. His eagerness to employ "special materials" has resulted in major trend-setting applications. Vassallo and his projects have been showcased in many television segments including an HGTV special.

The firm's project list includes pools for major hotels, casino moguls, celebrated chefs, celebrities, luxury home tours and multiple man-made lake renovations.

Vassallo serves on local, regional, and national boards for the Association of Pool and Spa Professionals (APSP), including the National Board of Directors Executive Committee. He is a past chairman of the Builders Council and the Builders Education Committee. He is also a contributor to the association's foremost technical publication, the *APSP Builders Manual 3rd Edition*.

One of few world-wide to earn the Certified Building Professional (CBP) credentials, this notes him as one of the pool industry's elite.

Vassallo has made a mark in the industry; he presents seminars for international symposiums, contributes to technical manuals, mentors novice designers and is a consultant to financial investors. He works with local, state and national legislators impacting licensing, standards, building codes, and safety regulations.

Considered one of the industry's thought leaders, he is sought by media, industry peers, legislatures, and building officials for advice on a wide range of topics from design to safety and regulatory issues. Highly editorialized, Vassallo is featured in publications across the globe. Former contributing columnist to Nevada's largest newspaper, the Las Vegas Review Journal, his column Pools and Spas provided readers with information on an array of pool and spa related subjects including construction, maintenance, entertainment and trends. He is currently the International Advisor and columnist for WAVES Magazine: India's pool, spa and bath publication.

He is the co-author of *The Al Fresco Life: Pools, Spas, Bars & Kitchens*, a design and lifestyle book exclusively featuring projects from the Paragon Pools portfolio.

Vassallo's company is the only independent builder in the state of Nevada to be named to the AQUA 100, the best pool companies in the nation, five years consecutively, and to the AQUA 100 Hall of Fame. The firm's designs have won a multitude of awards including Best Pool in the Las Vegas Parade of Homes, Master of Design by Pool and Spa News, HEIDI Awards Best Exterior, AQUA Choice Award, ADAS Best Pool, multiple APSP Awards of Excellence and Signature Pools & Spas Design Awards.

His humanitarian works involving educational and water safety programs have earned numerous accolades including Citizen of Distinction, The Jefferson Award, the Golden Hands Service Award and the Las Vegas Chamber of Commerce Entrepreneur of the Year. Vassallo is also a recipient of the Inspire Award and was named the 2012 APSP CBP of the Year.

MARY B. VAIL, OSG
Co-Founder, Three V Enterprises
President, Mary Vail, OSG, Publicist
Las Vegas, Nevada, USA
www.maryvailpublicist.com

An author, photographer, and publicist, Mary Vail is a public relations and marketing professional who has successfully placed clients in traditional and emerging media with notoriety in feature stories, images, coveted awards and accolades.

As founder and president of Mary Vail, OSG Publicist, an independent public relations firm, she specializes in image building campaigns and focuses her energies on "positive" publicity. The firm has designed and managed successful innovative campaigns for a vast array of organizations from aerospace, to entertainment, filmmaking, fine art, gaming, hospitality, homebuilding, medical, construction, sports marketing and more.

Her high-quality photographs have appeared in major publications, both electronic and print versions, and social media sites, providing a unique value-added service few publicists offer their clients. Additionally, she provides literary support as a "ghostwriter" and researcher: Vail has secured posts for clients with assignments as columnists, feature writers, and in editorial positions world-wide. In 2009, she teamed up with Joe M. Vassallo to co-author and publish a lifestyle and design book, The Al Fresco Life: Pools, Spas, Bars and Kitchens, for which she provided hundreds of images. Since then, she has gone on to co-author the *International Award-Winning Pools, Spas, and Water Environments* series, all under Schiffer Publishing.

Known as the "Philanthropic Publicist," Vail's humanitarian efforts have been the focus of her career: seeking ways to improve the educational, physical, and socio-economical lifestyle of those less fortunate. The esteemed publicist has been recognized locally, nationally, and internationally, garnering numerous awards and prestigious accolades: Knighthood in the Order of St. George-Knights of Malta; the Paul M. Lund Public Service Award, the highest individual community service award from the Public Relations Society of America; the Jefferson Award; the Key to the City of Las Vegas, as well as other awards, and numerous proclamations and congressional citations.

Vail has also received multiple design awards, including Addy Awards, MarCom Creative Design Awards, W3 Web Design Awards, and Davey Awards. Vail is a graduate of the University of Hawaii-Manoa and is currently enrolled in the EMBA program at the University of Nevada Las Vegas.

JOSEPH A. VASSALLO, CBP
Vice President, Paragon Pools
Las Vegas, Nevada, USA
www.paragonpoolslv.com

A veteran in the swimming pool industry, Vassallo has over twenty years experience in designing custom pools and spas.

Joe Jr.'s career began as an apprentice designer working alongside his father. His natural architectural talents became profoundly evident and soon found him working in the engineering department learning the technical elements of design. That position proved to be invaluable, giving him an opportunity to review designs by some of the top designers in the country. Taking what he learned from that experience and blending it with his own natural talents, Joe Jr. has developed his own unique artistic style of design. He has the ability to take simple lines and curves and join them into an art form worthy of a painted canvas.

Joe Jr.'s architectural skills help him conceive complete habitats whereby the pool, landscape, decking, patio, play area and even dog runs are designed together to give the yard a total harmonious appearance.

Together with his father, the duo has built Paragon Pools into a nationally recognized custom in-ground commercial and residential pool builder with trend setting applications.

His designs and collaborations have earned him top design awards, including the Las Vegas Parade of Homes Best Pool, Pool and Spa News Master of Design, *Aqua Magazine* AQUA Choice Award, and multiple APSP Awards of Excellence. He was named to the Top 40 Under 40 Top Young Professionals by *InBusiness Magazine*.

Joe Jr. earned the industry's elite Certified Building Professional (CBP) credentials presented by the Association of Pool and Spa Professionals (APSP). He also passed the Nevada State Contractors Board exam earning him the accreditation of Qualified Expert (QE) in the state.

Active in the industries professional association, Joe Jr. serves on the APSP Builders Education Committee.

THE ADVISORY BOARD

NOAH NEHLICH
Owner/Founder, Structure Studios
www.structurestudios.com

SEAN VAIL
Informatist/Consultant
seanvail@gmail.com

RON LACHER, P.E., CBP
Founder/President, Pool Engineering, Inc.
www.pooleng.com

BRETT LLOYD ABBOTT
Founder/ CEO, MYM Austin, Inc.
www.mymaustin.com

THE EDITORIAL STAFF

SEAN AMMERMAN
Editorial Assistant

ASHLEY VAIL
Editorial Assistant & Event Coordination